Original title:
Fern Fragments

Copyright © 2025 Creative Arts Management OÜ
All rights reserved.

Author: Penelope Hawthorne
ISBN HARDBACK: 978-1-80567-180-0
ISBN PAPERBACK: 978-1-80567-479-5

A Serenade for the Swaying

In the forest where leaves dance,
Nature's silly little prance.
Breezes tickle every stem,
Whispering secrets, a leafy gem.

Ferns in hats, a gala style,
Swirling around, they laugh awhile.
Crickets chirp in perfect tune,
While squirrels roll like feathered balloons.

Dancing roots with roots so spry,
Wave their limbs to the sky.
Mice join in, a tiny jig,
As the whole woods go big!

With playful twists and flippant fun,
Every leaf, a little pun.
When nature smiles, oh what a sight,
A cheeky show, sheer delight!

Solace in the Shade

In shadows cool, a lizard grins,
With sunburnt friends, he basks in sins.
A squirrel chatters, dressed in tweed,
He swears he's found that perfect seed.

The breeze brings whispers, tree leaves dance,
A mischief brew, a leaf-based trance.
Ants march in lines, a tiny parade,
With snacks galore, their feasts displayed.

Nature's Fragile Echoes

A bug with stripes, oh what a show,
Waltzes on petals, stealing the glow.
A butterfly winks, as if to say,
"Does this wing make my back look gay?"

A dandelion fluff floats on by,
It tickles the nose of a butterfly.
He sneezes so loud, all creatures jump,
A surprise for the ants, who start to thump.

Essence of Hidden Life

In grass blades sharp, a mouse makes soup,
While frogs critique, forming a troupe.
A toad croaks loudly, hoping for fame,
But gets overshadowed by a bird's game.

Worms have a conference, debating the rain,
In muddy discuss, they chant their refrain.
With heads in the soil, they laugh 'til they cry,
As raindrops like marbles, come tumbling by.

Phantoms of the Foliage

A ghostly fern floats, hardly a sound,
Witty and sneaky, it glides around.
It tickles a fawn, and off it does race,
As branches all giggle, the trees turn their face.

The whispers of leaves hold secrets untold,
As sprites play tag in the bright, green fold.
With laughter that echoes through meadow and glade,
They dance in a net of sunlight and shade.

Amongst the Green Guardians

In a jungle of leafy hats,
The plants wear shades and look so chitchat,
Whispering secrets to a wandering bee,
While squirrels giggle at their own esprit.

Tall trees boast of their leafy stashes,
Claiming they're royalty, while everyone clashes,
A cactus tells tales of a sunny retreat,
And laughter echoes with each little beat.

Fleeting Moments in the Shade

Underneath the leafy porch,
A toad croaks jokes as he does a torch,
While shadows play tag in a vibrant spree,
With wiggly worms jumping out to see.

The sun dips low, a playful tease,
As ladybugs chill in the gentle breeze,
Caterpillars schmooze in polka-dot suits,
With a punchline waiting in sprightly roots.

The Dance of Delicate Growth

Frogs in bow ties take center stage,
As daisies and dandelions set the page,
Twisting and twirling in a verdant swirl,
While petals and pollen join in the whirl.

A sprightly breeze plays the violin,
As mushrooms boogie, inviting a spin,
With fireflies flashing as disco lights,
It's a wild party on warm summer nights.

Adrift in the Woodland

A chipmunk in stripes hosts a grand feast,
As acorns are juggled by a playful beast,
Squirrels try to breakdance on a new trend,
While mushrooms crack jokes that they cannot send.

Rooted in giggles, the trees shake their limbs,
Sharing tall tales of their whimsical whims,
A turtle slow-claps, pretending to cheer,
As nature chuckles, it's crystal clear.

Textures of Time in Thickets

In a thicket, leaves do play,
Hiding secrets in shades of gray.
Time tickles the bark so bold,
Whispers of stories yet untold.

Squirrels dress up in leafy attire,
Planning heists near the campfire.
Raccoons in masks, quite the scene,
Plotting mischief, all so keen!

Nature's Whispering Manuscript

The trees scribble notes on the breeze,
Tickling toes of honeybees.
Crickets compose a nightly score,
While owls provide the encore.

A snail sends love letters in slime,
Each word a slow dance with time.
Porcupines writing tales of woe,
Prickly but cute, don't you know?

Veins of an Ancient World

Roots weave stories underground,
Ancient spirits all around.
A worm recites its history,
In the mud, such a mystery!

Mushrooms gossip, cozy and bright,
Sharing secrets through the night.
Listening in, the wise old oak,
Chuckles softly, never a joke.

Choreography of Shadows and Light

Sunbeams tango with the tree,
Twisting, turning, oh so free.
Shadows slide with a silly grin,
As the forest's dance begins.

Grasshopper leads with a hop and skip,
While beetles do a little flip.
Nature's stage in full delight,
A comical show, what a sight!

Spirals of Nature's Memory

In the forest, who's to say,
A leaf whispered loud, 'I'm on holiday!'
Dancing in winds, a playful spree,
While squirrels chuckled beneath the tree.

Beneath the sun, they twirl and tease,
"Watch out for bees! Let's not get squeezed!"
Frogs leap high, with a splash and grin,
Nature's jesters, where fun begins.

Echoing Nature's Silhouettes

Wobbly shadows jump on the ground,
'They're double-takers!' the crickets sound.
Mice in tuxedos in a mad dash,
Tiptoeing past the trash can stash.

Twisting vines giggle, 'We're not a chore!'
'We're in a dance-off, come join the floor!'
With glowing mushrooms throwing a bash,
Even the stones join in, roots to clash.

Lattice of Light and Leaf

The sun peeked through like a playful cat,
Looking for mischief, where's it at?
Bumbles buzzing with a comic flair,
Trip on petals, take care, beware!

Dandelions laugh, it's a puffy show,
Puffs soft as whispers, 'Come play, let's go!'
Nature's jests swirl like confetti bright,
Each corner holds a giggle, pure delight.

Fractals of Forgotten Forests

The trunks are twisted, a riddle to see,
"What's the secret?" they chuckle with glee.
Roots intertwine, hold a ticklish charm,
While owls hoot jokes, causing much alarm!

Vines dangle low, a prank on the ground,
Hiding from rabbits who leap all around.
With mushrooms peeping, they whisper, 'Oh dear!'
The laughter of trees is all we can hear!

Woven Secrets of the Bloom

In the garden where gnomes play,
A cabbage wearing glasses sways.
With carrots debating who's the best,
The radish claims he's passed the test.

A tulip tells a joke so neat,
But daisies can't get up off their feet.
As bees hum tunes of summer songs,
The onions giggle, 'This can't be wrong!'

Emerald Reveries

The leaves are chatting, don't you know,
They gossip while the breezes blow.
A worm on stilts, what a sight!
He dances, twirling, day and night.

A mushroom in a tuxedo stands,
With fungi friends and outstretched hands.
The moss replays its favorite jam,
While crickets snap, 'Hey, look at Sam!'

The Breath of Forest Spirits

In the woods, where shadows play,
A squirrel juggles acorns every day.
With owls that laugh at every blunder,
And raccoons plotting, what a wonder!

The river sings its silly song,
While frogs dance the whole night long.
A fox in shades says, 'I'm the boss!'
The rabbits hop, 'Oh dear, we're lost!'

Nature's Tarnished Mirror

Reflecting puddles show a clown,
With daisies wearing frowns upside down.
A bear in slippers struts with pride,
While chipmunks snicker from the side.

The sun throws rays without a care,
As butterflies do pirouettes in the air.
A breeze says, 'Oops, sorry for that!'
While ladybugs laugh at a rogue old hat.

Enchanted Veins of the Wild

In the woods where whispers creep,
Fuzzy greens in tangled heaps,
Leaves parade with mischief bright,
Dancing in the morning light.

Mossy hats on squirrels' heads,
Chatting with the sleepy beds,
Giggling roots beneath the trees,
Tickled by the swaying breeze.

The Language of Lushness

Plants gossip in leafy tones,
Telling tales of hidden bones,
With winks and wiggles, all in jest,
Creating laughs at nature's fest.

Frogs croak in a ribbit rhyme,
As daisies dance in perfect time,
A chorus fills the air so bright,
Nature's jesters in delight.

Verdant Verses Hidden Below

Underneath the ground so low,
Worms compose a secret show,
Giggles from the rooty crew,
Composing tunes from soil dew.

Toadstools cheer for passing bugs,
In their hats, they play with shrugs,
A party brews, a joyful sigh,
As fireflies twinkle in the sky.

Mosaics of the Forest Floor

Patchwork carpet, colors blend,
Each petal plays a cheeky friend,
With dandelions in their crown,
They giggle as the winds blow down.

Geckos strut with tiny flair,
Waving tales of forest air,
In this stunning leafy hall,
Nature holds the grandest ball.

Veils of Resilience

In the shadows, green hats sit,
Hiding secrets, a leafy wit.
With a wiggle and a twist,
Nature's prank, we can't resist.

Dancing roots in silly prance,
A foliage glee, a leafy dance.
They whisper tales in rustling cheer,
A giggle here, a snicker near.

Racing vines with jokes to tell,
Creeping up the garden well.
They sprout like laughter in the sun,
Growing wild, it's all in fun!

Oh, those greens, with sneaky charm,
Wrapped around like nature's arm.
Their jokes are wrapped in chlorophyll,
In the woodland, humor's thrill.

Threads of Silent Growth

In the quiet, whispers bloom,
Tails of green, they create a room.
With a nod, they spin and weave,
Nature's quirks, we can't believe.

Twisting right, then to the left,
Like little gnomes, they're quite bereft.
Branches giggle as they sway,
Telling tales of yesterday.

Mossy hats and shady smiles,
Growing cheeky for a while.
They tiptoe through the dew-lit morn,
Laughter sprouting, fresh and worn.

As sunlight drips from skies so blue,
They plot the garden's next debut.
In this weave of green delight,
Every thread's a joyous sight.

Breaths of the Wooded Realm

A burble here, a leafy sigh,
Whispers echo, oh my, oh my!
The woods chuckle in playful tones,
With knobby roots and weathered stones.

Breezes play the funny flute,
While woodland critters dance astute.
Acorns bounce like laughing beans,
In a world where humor leans.

Twisting trunks with hidden glee,
Carving jokes in barks, you see.
Branches break into silly fits,
Tickling leaves with creamy wits.

As shadows play, the sun ticks slow,
A game of hide-and-seek they know.
In the wooded realm, laughter swings,
Nature's heart, where joy springs.

Green Memories in the Wind

Whispers swirl in breezy flight,
A splash of green, a joke in sight.
The winds carry tales, so bright,
Of garden laughs and songs of light.

Petals giggle, swaying low,
Tickling thoughts, they put on a show.
Each gust tugs at leafy veils,
Confessions shared in silken trails.

Dandelions puff with glee,
Scattering laughs for all to see.
They tumble down in playful spins,
And scatter joy as their tale begins.

In the silence, memories hum,
Of playful days when nature's fun.
The winds take flight, a green parade,
In this canvas where jokes are laid.

The Delicate Balance

In a garden where chaos reigns,
A squirrel steals snacks, calls it gains.
The daisies giggle, the tulips tease,
While bees dance wildly on a summer breeze.

A worm in a hat thinks it's quite grand,
Sporting a wig made of rubber band.
While snails race slowly, the rabbits sigh,
As they hear the crow's peculiar cry.

Thorns whisper secrets to the spring air,
While ladybugs hide, pretending to care.
Each leaf winks, in playful jest,
Nature's circus puts humor to the test.

Breezes are ninjas, sneaking about,
Chasing the laughter, causing a shout.
In this world of green, fun's a must,
Nature's pranksters—oh, how they trust!

Reveries in Green

Leaves play poker under the bright sun,
Telling tall tales of a race just for fun.
The roots giggle as they dig deep,
While ants debate where to pile their heap.

Whispers of grass tickle the toes,
As butterflies wear their fanciest clothes.
A beetle breaks out dancing with flair,
Turning the garden into a fair.

The shadows throw shade, acting all cool,
While sunlight sparkles—a sparkling pool.
Nature composes its wittiest tune,
With laughter that's brighter than the afternoon.

With stems that shimmy and petals that sway,
Every day's a festival—hip hip hooray!
In the arms of green, the humor's supreme,
Life here's a whimsical, wild dream!

Canopy Layers

Up in the trees, where the squirrels convene,
Their acorn debates are quite often obscene.
With chattering laughter and raucous delight,
The branches join in, putting up a fight.

The owls roll their eyes at the sheer display,
While mockingbirds croon, come out, and play.
Each leaf holds a secret, a whispered joke,
Even the shadows begin to provoke.

A raccoon in pajamas starts a small brawl,
As butterflies flutter—oh what a ball!
In this leafy layer, the gags never end,
Each creature's a joker, each branch is a friend.

So when you look up, and the leafy dance sways,
Know that in laughter, the forest plays.
With humor aloft, and a wink from the sun,
Nature's a stage, and we're all here for fun!

Fronds in Twilight

As twilight falls, the critters prepare,
For a grand night under starlit glare.
The fireflies flicker like lamps on parade,
While laughter echoes in shadows displayed.

In the hush of dusk, the crickets compose,
A symphony sweet as they serenade rose.
An opossum in bowtie, so dapper, so proud,
Takes center stage, gathers quite the crowd.

The moon rolls its eyes at this nightly affair,
While mushrooms cheerlead with flair and with care.
"Life's just a dance, a whimsical show!"
The earthworms cheer from their home down below.

With giggles and wiggles, the night stretches on,
Under twinkling stars where the magic is drawn.
In this feast of fun, all creatures unite,
For laughter and joy—what a wondrous sight!

Frayed Edges of Nature

A leaf once crisp, now a frayed edge,
Waving like it's lost a hedge.
Insects peek and take a bite,
Who knew salad could take flight?

Soggy ground makes for slippery fun,
Nature's game, come join the run!
A squirrel snickers, jumps with glee,
While the snail thinks, 'That's so me!'

Twisted roots, like knotted hair,
Causing all to stop and stare.
A chipmunk dances in the breeze,
Chasing buddies through the trees.

So come retrace each mystic path,
Evoking in you endless laughs.
In nature's zoo, we lose all stress,
With tangled vines, who could guess?

Beneath the Canopy

Under green umbrellas, shadows play,
Frogs are croaking 'Hey, Hooray!'.
Mushrooms hold a waltzing show,
While the daisies blush and glow.

The air's a mix of must and fun,
Feeling like a sticky bun.
Spiders spinning webs with flair,
Are they building or just a lair?

A raccoon tries to take a sip,
But slips and gives a comedic trip.
Birds gossip about the day's scheme,
While a lost ant just wants ice cream.

The leaves above wear hats of rain,
Nature's antics, absurd but plain.
Each twist and turn holds a surprise,
Beneath the greenery, laughter flies.

Lush Remnants of the Past

Once a forest, now a tale,
Of a tree that tried to sail.
Saplings giggle, reaching up,
"Grab that breeze, it's time to sup!"

Old logs now host a vibrant crew,
Where critters plot and giggle too.
Mushrooms hugging each crooked stump,
Watch out! They may give you a jump!

An oak stands tall, with tales to share,
Of cheeky squirrels and breeze so rare.
Each branch a storyteller's dream,
Life's wacky joy is but a theme.

Leaves murmur when the winds depart,
Nature's jesters play their part.
In every nook and hidden stash,
Laughter echoes with a splash.

Cradle of the Forest

In the cradle where the wild things sleep,
Ferns and fungi form a heap.
A bunny hops with floppy ears,
While the owl giggles through the years.

The sun peeks through with a cheeky glare,
Whispering secrets for those who dare.
A tortoise moves with the grace of a dance,
While the newts take a chance on romance!

Crickets chirp their rhythmic jest,
In nature's carnival, they're the best.
Tree trunks chat about the years,
With laughter mingling, brushing fears.

Every shadow holds a wink,
With whispers of what's deep in sync.
So roam this playground, wide and free,
In the cradle, come laugh with me!

Sylvan Secrets in Green

In the woods, a squirrel twirled,
Chasing tales that leaves unfurled.
A rabbit danced but tripped on roots,
Said, "I've got two left feet for boots!"

Tiny bugs do waltzes neat,
While ants march to a buzzing beat.
Their secret dance, a sight to see,
They'll start a trend, just wait for me!

A deer stepped in while laughing loud,
Wearing a crown of acorn proud.
"Let's start a fashion show, oh dear!"
Said all the critters, filled with cheer.

The trees all giggled, branches swayed,
As silly shadows danced and played.
What secrets in this green abode?
Laughter leaps while mischief's sowed!

Celestial Patterns of the Thicket

Stars peek through the leafy veil,
While owls hoot a whimsical tale.
A raccoon's juggling acorns bright,
Said, "I'm the king of moonlit night!"

The bushes whisper, secrets shared,
With every tangled branch declared.
A fox in shades of crafty green,
Claims, "I'm the prettiest you've seen!"

Fireflies flicker like tiny stars,
Holding parties near the jars.
Glow worms dance in a lovely groove,
Swaying to rhythms that make you move!

With laughter echoing, sounds delight,
The thicket bursts with sheer delight.
Under the sky, with hearts so bold,
Funny tales in the night unfold!

Beneath the Canopy's Embrace

Under leaves where shadows play,
A turtle says, "I'll race today!"
A snail laughs, "You'll win by dusk,
I'm still stuck in this leafy husk!"

Mice skitter on a crumb of bread,
One says, "I'll use this for my bed!"
The crumbs turn into a cozy loft,
As bunnies leap, saying, "Alfie, scoff!"

A bear joins in, with a silly grin,
Spinning round till he falls in.
"Now that's a dance, take my advice,
A tumble here is worth the price!"

Vines twist and turn in quirky ways,
Leaves shake as they bow and sway.
In this green abode, all is chuckled,
Life's a jolly game, unfettered!

Sunlight Paints the Undergrowth

Sunshine drips through branches wide,
Painting patches where shadows hide.
A lizard basks, feels oh-so-fine,
Says, "I'm sunbathing—with a twist of lime!"

Daisies argue, who's the fairest bloom,
While a bee buzzes, adding to the room.
"You're all cute, I'll take my pick,
But I'm off to find a honey tick!"

The mushrooms giggle, "Look at this!"
One says, "I'll grant you a tasty kiss!"
But the gnome frowned, as he stood tall,
"Magic shrooms! Don't eat them at all!"

Sunlight dances on leaves so bright,
Creating laughter, pure delight.
In undergrowth where fun abounds,
Funny creatures prance without bounds!

Nature's Hidden Portraits

In the glade where shadows play,
Mushrooms wear a funny hat,
A squirrel claims to run the show,
While the insects tip their spat.

Lichen laughs upon the bark,
Whispers of a forest prank,
A rabbit with a hidden quirk,
Dances in the twilight dank.

The leaves are chatting up a storm,
Sharing secrets on the breeze,
While a hawk makes a dramatic swoop,
Scaring off a pair of bees.

Oh, the fables that unfold,
Under branches, twist, and twine,
Nature's humor, bright and bold,
In her canvas, we entwine.

Tales from the Woodland Depths

In the depth of shade and cheer,
A fox slips on an old banana,
Chuckling at a deer so near,
Who's stuck in a dance of a tanna.

A wise old owl hoots with glee,
As shadows tickle the ground,
He tells tales of absurdity,
In rhythms that astound.

Little mice hold a debate,
Arguing over cheese and cake,
While beetles race and speculate,
Who will win this grand mistake?

Nature's jesters gather round,
In a realm where laughter breeds,
A woodland vibe where joy is found,
Among the gossip of the leaves.

The Alchemy of Shade and Sun

Dancing light upon the floor,
Toadstools skip in summer's air,
Bumblebees might start a war,
Over honey, sweet and rare.

With a chuckle and a twist,
A chipmunk steals the scene once more,
He feigns to be a forest myst,
But forgets he closed the door.

Shadows play a game of chase,
Behind a kooky, crooked tree,
Sunbeams giggle, their embrace,
Turns the grass into a spree.

Nature's whimsy, pure delight,
In the mix of dark and light,
Turns the forest into jest,
Where every creature feels the best.

Interwoven Histories of Green

Once a leaf dropped, stars did grin,
As it spun a tale of old,
A caterpillar wore a fin,
While the moss remained so bold.

Crickets shared their quirkiest lore,
Underneath the tangled brush,
A worm, with dreams, began to soar,
In the night, he made a hush.

Branches looped in laughter's hug,
Tickling roots in a jest,
Where every twig and tiny bug,
Knew how to throw a fest.

Through the dance of leaves and vine,
History whispers all around,
In the laughter, oh so fine,
Nature's jokes are tightly bound.

Fractal Patterns in Green

In a world of leafy jig,
Where patterns twist and twirl,
I found a dance with roots so big,
That silliness began to swirl.

Their shapes are quite absurd,
Like hats on cats, you see,
Each leaf a frilly word,
In nature's own decree.

A puzzle made of greens,
That tickles every thought,
It's where the laughter beans,
Brought smiles that can't be bought.

In the garden's sunny space,
I lost my sense of time,
Chasing shapes in a happy race,
Each turn was a little rhyme.

Subtle Green Murmurs

Listen close, the leaves all giggle,
In whispers soft and bright,
A secret dance, a gentle wiggle,
Beneath the beams of light.

The bushes chatter, oh so sly,
With stories of the sun,
While shadows bounce and fly,
With mischief just for fun.

A rustling breeze, a playful nudge,
The vines all twist and sway,
They tease me, oh, I just can't budge,
Into their leafy play.

Amidst the emerald cheers,
I chuckled at my plight,
For every giggle shifts my gears,
And makes the day feel light.

Tinctures of Life

In hues of green, the world's a joke,
With splashes here and there,
A watercolor—oh what a poke!
With pranks hiding in the air.

The dandelions wear crowns of fluff,
Dancing jesters on the lawn,
They tickle me and that's enough,
With laughter spilling on and on.

A palette filled with life's own cheer,
From sprout to stalk, they tease,
In nature's art, I find no fear,
Just chuckles in the breeze.

Each patch of grass, a sordid tale,
Of mischief, fun, and green,
Where every twist and turn prevails,
In this lush, silly scene.

Grove of Forgotten Tales

In a grove where giggles dwell,
The branches sway with glee,
Whispering secrets, oh so swell,
    Of stories wild and free.

Here, mushrooms wear the silliest hats,
While squirrels jest and play,
The snickering blooms of quirky spats,
    Color the bright bouquet.

Among the trunks, a riddle hums,
Tickling the passerby,
Nature's antics—see how it thrums,
    Beneath the azure sky.

So join the fun, don't be shy,
In this woodland's joyful leap,
For every chuckle makes the tie,
    Of laughter, oh so deep.

The Hidden Symphony of Leaves

In the forest, leaves hold a tune,
Dancing lightly to a cheerful croon.
Squirrels tap-dance on branches high,
While the owls hoot, feeling spry.

Tiny frogs play the silent bass,
While raccoons juggle in a race.
Mice compose with a whispering breeze,
In this concert, nothing aims to please.

The wind joins in as a raucous friend,
Mixing up chaos that won't quite end.
Sunshine beams, a spotlight bright,
Casting shadows in a playful light.

Nature's laughter is heard all around,
In each rustle, joy can be found.
Tickling roots and teasing bark,
This is fun in the woodland park.

Green Dreams in a Dappled Realm

Once I dreamed of hats made of leaves,
Wore one to a party, oh how it deceives!
Frogs croaked songs of bittersweet plight,
As turtles danced under the moonlight.

Mushrooms stood in line, wanting to shine,
As ants marched by, forming a line.
A snail rolled by on a slippery spree,
Claiming the best seat by the old tree.

Laughter echoes through trunks so wide,
While the insects play hide and seek beside.
Each leaf whispers tales with a chuckle here,
As ladybugs cheer on, full of cheer!

Wandering through greenery so fine,
Life's peculiar theater, a comedy line.
Sticks become wands of magical feats,
In this green dreamland, no one retreats.

Patterns of Life Among the Moss

A dance on the moss, what a sight to behold,
Where critters gather, both brave and bold.
A hedgehog in slippers took a long stroll,
While worms laughed softly, digging their hole.

Ants held a banquet, crumbs everywhere,
While spiders spun webs with intricate flair.
In clumps of green, there's giggles that rise,
As beetles roll marbles 'neath the blue skies.

Fungi with hats throw a mushroom ball,
Toadstools are benches, a party for all.
Rhythmic tapping from the woodpecker's chase,
Echoes the laughter, brings joy to the space.

Life weaves a dance, with patterns galore,
Each creature contributing more and more.
In vibrant hues, the antics unfold,
With moss as a stage, where stories are told.

Beneath the Earth's Fern-Like Breath

Beneath the ground, things twist and turn,
With roots laughing while the seedlings yearn.
A worm in a bow tie gives a grand speech,
Claiming the underground is within reach.

Gophers play poker, chips made of seeds,
While crickets lace dance shoes fit for their needs.
Earth's warm breath puffs up with pride,
As rascals of soil sneak out to hide.

Puddles of water hold echoes of glee,
As gravel road songs hum blissfully.
Down there, the secrets are silly and bold,
Waiting for stories of laughter to unfold.

From dandelion seeds to the whiskers of mice,
Every little creature, a gift that's precise.
In the humor of roots, they all intertwine,
Beneath the earth's breath, all things align.

Whispers of Green Shadows

In a garden where odd plants play,
A leaf sneezed, and took flight, hooray!
The flowers giggled, oh what a sight,
As the stem tripped over, in pure delight.

A snail in shades, sips tea on a leaf,
Says, "I'm faster!" — oh, what a belief!
The daisies chuckled, they couldn't stop,
As the gentle breeze gave the mushrooms a hop.

The sun tickled stems with a warm embrace,
While shadows danced with a cheeky grace.
The vines, they tangled in a festive knot,
Who knew foliage had such a lot?

In this green world, mischief's the theme,
A tree bursts out laughing, what a grand scheme!
When petals fall, like confetti in flight,
The garden erupts, oh what pure delight!

Echoes in the Underbrush

In the underbrush, a berry wore shoes,
Dancing along with whimsical blues.
A chubby toad croaked out a tune,
While bugs did the cha-cha beneath the moon.

A squirrel proclaimed, with a wink and a spin,
"Who needs nuts? We feast on wild gin!"
The mushrooms, they twirled in a jazzy display,
As the owl dropped beats, hip-hop for the hay.

Leaves rustled loudly, talking some smack,
While vines tangled up on a sneaky snaketrack.
The bushes erupted with laughter and cheer,
For in this wild place, there's nothing to fear.

Beneath the soft light of a flickering fire,
A critter ballet, oh how they aspire!
With each little stomp, they stomped out a rhyme,
In this rambunctious jungle, they're having a time!

Luminous Leaf Tapestry

In a world where sunlight had flair,
Leaves giggled secrets, like they didn't care.
Waving their hands like they were on stage,
This leafy tapestry turned a new page.

A chattering crow plotted a prank,
Dressed as a leaf, he scampered and sank.
The daisies gave laughter, a riotous show,
While crickets debated, should they join the flow?

A quirky mushroom turned fuchsia in glee,
While the fireflies swayed, so wild and free.
The branches swayed, with a rustle of jest,
Declaring by far that they were the best!

With petals like ribbons, they danced in the wind,
Each gust of fresh laughter, a twist and a spin.
In this vibrant dream, where the green things play,
The joyous light shines, come join the display!

Secrets of the Shaded Grove

In the shaded grove, where giggles unfold,
A wise old tree told jokes, oh so bold.
"Why did the seed refuse to grow tall?
It heard the weeds were having a ball!"

The ferns held their breath, trying not to chime,
But snickered and snorted, breaking the rhyme.
While sleepy beetles watched with wide eyes,
At the punchline delivered, they burst into sighs.

A gopher, in glasses, read tales from a book,
With a title so long, no one dared look.
"In the land of roots, and the realm of the leaf,
Where laughter's the currency, there's no room for grief!"

In laughter, they spun, from dusk until dawn,
Every shadow was dancing, a jubilant spawn.
So come to this grove, with secrets to see,
Where fun's in abundance, and all can agree!

Fernlike Silhouettes

In shadows deep, they dance and prance,
With leafy hats, they lead the chance.
A twist, a zoom, oh look at them go,
Nature's green jesters, stealing the show.

Their stems a joke, so wobbly and spry,
Who knew plants could be so sly?
With playful curls, they share a grin,
And flap around as if to win.

In every nook, a sneak peek here,
With whispered giggles that tickle the ear.
They rustle secrets, they tumble and flip,
In this leafy realm, no one takes a trip!

As evening falls, the jokes do not cease,
They scatter light and bring such peace.
In silent chuckles, they fade from sight,
The day's green jesters, off into night.

Nature's Whispering Pages

In the library of leaves, a tale unfurls,
With stories spun by sprightly swirls.
Each leaf a page, curled tight with glee,
Whispering laughter from tree to tree.

'Oh look!' they snicker, 'another lost bug!'
Stuck in a web, just giving a shrug.
Their giggles ripple through branches wide,
While bugs in crisis try to hide.

'This chapter's wild, you won't believe it!'
Nature's book with a comedic twist.
The sunbeam melts as the pages flip,
With every rustle, another quip!

So come take a peek, oh wondrous friend,
In this leafy library that never ends.
With giggles and whispers from plants on the stage,
Together we dance through nature's pages.

The Heart of the Glade

In the glade of giggles, where laughter grows,
Mischievous plants strike their funny pose.
With roots like ribbons and leaves that twirl,
They spin in circles, like nature's whirl.

A gnome in the corner lifts an eyebrow high,
As flowers burst forth and go "Oh my!"
A butterfly winks, "Care to join the spree?"
With floral confetti, they dance with glee.

A crooked stick adds a comedic flair,
As toadstools gather with a fanciful air.
They chatter and chirp, those plants full of zest,
In the heart of the glade, they're truly the best!

So let's join the frolic, let worries retreat,
In this joyous thicket, life's a treat.
Where laughter echoes and fun finds a way,
In the heart of the glade, forever we'll stay.

A Symphony of Shadows

Beneath the trees, where shadows flounce,
A symphony plays, oh what a bounce!
With leafy instruments, they serenade,
Each rustle a giggle, an earthbound parade.

The sunbeams laugh, playing peek-a-boo,
While shadows sway in a ridiculous cue.
A squirrel joins in, tapping his feet,
With acorn maracas, oh what a treat!

In this wild orchestra, no tune is bland,
With giggling branches, and nature's hand.
The melody's light, like a feather it drifts,
As critters and plants share their funny gifts.

When the dusk draws near, our concert will end,
But laughter lingers, as shadows descend.
In this symphony sweet, we've had our play,
With nature and jest, who needs a ballet?

Secrets Cradled in Nature's Hand

In the whispering woods, secrets hide,
A squirrel wearing glasses, quite the guide.
With acorns in pockets, he does prance,
Pondering life in a woodland dance.

A frog with a crown croaks out jokes,
Telling the trees of silly folks.
Mice in tuxedos serve cheese on a plate,
While dancing in rhythm, they celebrate fate.

Butterflies gossip, gaily they flit,
Trading tall tales, a real comedic hit.
The owls hoot laughter in bemused delight,
While fireflies twinkle, turning day into night.

Dances of Shadows in Woodland Silence

In the moonlight glow, shadows join the play,
A wabbit with shoes decides to sway.
With each little hop, he tries to fly,
But trips on a twig with a comical cry.

Tree trunks are laughing, their bark worn and wise,
As raccoons juggle nuts, much to our surprise.
With a wink and a nod, they drop all their food,
Creating a scene that's quite merry and crude.

Beneath the old oaks, a party unfolds,
Where laughter grows wild and whimsy beholds.
The shadows keep dancing, and moonbeams keep cheer,
In this vibrant forest, joy's always near.

Whispers of the Green Veil

Under leafy curtains, secrets do sing,
A turtle on stilts claims he's the king.
With a wink from a rabbit, and giggles abound,
They dance in a circle, spinning round and round.

A snake in a top hat recites silly rhymes,
While crickets play music in playful chimes.
Moss-covered benches invite friends to sit,
Where laughter erupts in a forest of wit.

The bushes are chuckling, the brambles conspire,
With shadows that wiggle, and thoughts that inspire.
Together they celebrate under the trees,
In a whimsical world that flutters with ease.

Echoes in the Underbrush

In the underbrush whispers, a joke takes flight,
A hedgehog with glasses declares, 'I'm quite bright!'
With a roll and a chuckle, he bounces along,
While ladybugs sing him a humorous song.

Dandelions giggle as they puff and blow,
Each seed a wish for a fun-loving show.
Beneath fuzzy mushrooms, the creatures convene,
Where the punchlines are plenty and laughter is seen.

Frogs leap in rhythm, joining the fun,
Hiding in the leaves, they bask in the sun.
With whispers of joy that dance through the night,
Echoes of laughter take feathered flight.

Lattice of Leaves

In a patch of green they hide,
A leaf at the front, one behind.
Whispering secrets of the breeze,
Pretending they're part of the trees.

With sun hats made of dew and lace,
They giggle in their leafy space.
A dance-off with the ants below,
A waltz that steals the woodland show.

But when the rain begins to fall,
They hold their breath, they fear it all.
For in their frenzy, oh what a scene,
They turn to mush like unseen cuisine!

Yet when the sun returns with cheer,
Out come the leaves, not a worry, no fear.
With laughter that rustles through the glade,
In their lively court, the dance parade!

Secrets of the Woodland Floor

What lies beneath the towering trees,
Are giggly roots and buzzing bees.
They plot and plan a grand parade,
With tiny hats that sunlight made.

One mushroom speaks with quite a flair,
"Look at my cap, the finest wear!"
While beetles march with tiny drums,
Their rhythm makes the forest hums.

But when the owl gives a sleepy nod,
They all play tricks, oh how they prod!
"Let's scare the deer, we'll wear a mask,
A game of hide and seek, a playful task!"

A tickle from the sappy pine,
An invitation for a fun dine.
They share a feast of fallen fries,
With laughter lifting to the skies!

Shattered Moss Dreams

Once a soft bed for gnomes to nap,
Now shattered dreams in a mossy flap.
The squirrels play games of hide and seek,
While mushrooms giggle, hiding their beak.

"Betcha I can hop higher than you!"
The brave toad boasts, it's quite the view.
But landing on soft moss is a curse,
Ends with a splash and a funny verse.

The ants with plans minding their biz,
Shake their heads at this droll quiz.
While ladybugs laugh, "Oh what a sight,
Toads in the air, now that's delight!"

In this forest where dreams take flight,
Even the shadows chuckle at night.
For in the chaos of greens and browns,
Are puddles of laughter, and giggly clowns!

The Fern's Silent Soliloquy

In silence, stands a leafy throng,
Speaking in whispers, but not for long.
They chuckle at grasses, so prim and neat,
With wavy fronds dancing to their own beat.

"Who needs a flower?" one boldly said,
"When I can wear a crown atop my head?"
The picnic ants shake their tiny heads,
"Just be careful of what you tread!"

As squirrels take bets on who will fall,
The leaves play cards, with laughter to sprawl.
"Two acorns please for a turn of fate,
Let's make this a game, it's never too late!"

So here in the hush of the woodland fair,
Even the sighs become jokes of air.
For in their secrets, the humor flows,
In a world where the laughter never slows!

The Soft Touch of Green

In the garden, leaves dance around,
A tickle and tease on the ground.
One snack found, a bug on my toe,
I jump up quick, 'Oh no, oh no!'

Lush is the pillow where bunnies lay,
But watch where you step, don't cause dismay.
A friendly snail gives me a wink,
As I ponder how they never stink.

Each sprout a tale, every blade a jest,
Some plants lounge, others play dress.
The grass says, 'Hey, join in the fun!'
But one swift sneeze… oh, there goes my run!

As I frolic through this green domain,
I slip on a leaf, it's quite the strain.
Yet laughter follows behind my fall,
Nature's punchline, I'm having a ball!

Patterns of Nature's Kin

Leaves spiral round like spaghetti strands,
I try to catch them with clumsy hands.
A spider grins from a leafy booth,
I promise him, 'I'm not a sleuth!'

Grass blades gossip, they wiggle and sway,
'Who wore it best? You or Jay?'
I laugh at their chatter, that rich refrain,
While munching on snacks that bring no disdain.

Dandelions pop up, a riot of cheer,
Their yellow crowns make everything clear.
But don't blow them away, or you'll invoke,
The winds of chaos, and quite the joke!

Nature's a clown with some witty flair,
Each bump and twist a surprise to share.
Amidst the green, I can't help but grin,
These patterns of life are where fun begins!

Silhouettes Against the Light

Sunrise plays games with shadows so sweet,
I chase them and tumble, oh what a feat!
A bird calls out, 'Don't look now, friend!'
But I jump and shout, 'This joy has no end!'

With weeds as my pals, we twirl and spin,
Pretending we're dancers, let the fun begin!
I fall on a twig, and it snaps with a crack,
Nature claps back, my grace under attack!

A silhouette stretches, all thin and tall,
Feeling quite grand, though just in the fall.
But a breezy gust gives my wiggle a shove,
I tumble down laughing, it's nature I love!

Against the light, where shadows ignite,
The world is a stage, everything feels right.
With giggles and whispers, I bob and I weave,
In this funny dance, I just won't leave!

Entwined in Nature's Grasp

Among the branches, I swing with glee,
A squirrel says, 'Hey, you're copying me!'
I shrug and grin, 'Just sharing the dream,'
While dodging a twig—that's part of the theme!

Vines wrap around in a playful embrace,
Like nature's own hug in this leafy space.
A lizard stops short for a bite of my shoe,
I smile and tease, 'That's not food for you!'

Mushrooms pop up, each face a delight,
They giggle and wiggle in soft morning light.
I try to join in, but they roll away,
Guess mushrooms have manners, what can I say?

In nature's weird humor, we're all intertwined,
Every twist has a punchline, every leaf has its kind.
So let's sway and spin, in this wild green space,
Where laughter abounds, at our own little pace!

The Restoration of Green

In a pot on my sill, the leaves do dance,
With a wiggle and jiggle, they take a chance.
A sip of some sunlight, a drop of some rain,
They sprout out of nowhere, like they're full of champagne.

The cat gives a stare, with a skeptical eye,
As I whisper sweet nothings, they're my little allies.
They nod in agreement, it's a leafy affair,
While the dog's unimpressed and just sits there to glare.

We've got a small army of green on the way,
Waging wars on dust bunnies, ready to play.
Each leaf is a teammate, we're crafting our scene,
With laughter and mischief, oh what a routine!

So here's to my plants, the green hilarity,
They brighten my days, a leafy variety.
With roots in the silly, and stems in the fun,
We're a wacky old crew, under the warm sun.

Breathless in the Bower

In the nook of the garden, a tangle of dreams,
Where shadows are playful and sunlight redeems.
I stumble on roots, and my balance is gone,
A pirouette awkward, I land on the lawn.

The daisies are snickering, the roses all grin,
As I chase after breezes, my head in a spin.
The vines overhead weave a blanket of green,
I'm breathless from laughter; what a silly scene!

The critters all giggle, they hide and they peek,
While I'm tripping on petals, so light, yet so sleek.
The foliage chuckles; it gives me a cheer,
In this bower of joy, I've got nothing to fear.

So here in this mess, where the green wordplay grows,
My heart's filled with giggles, and everybody knows.
The plants have a knack for mischief and fun,
In this breathless escapade, we're never outdone!

The Emerald Lining

In the patch of my garden where green meets the sky,
There's a mystery brewing, oh my, oh my!
The peas plot an escape, the squash takes a dive,
While the carrots are giggling, it's alive, what a jive!

Twirling and spinning, they're organizing parades,
The cucumbers rumble, while the lettuce cascades.
I swoop in with snacks, a grand feast from my hand,
They nibble in chorus, a flavorful band.

The pumpkins are scheming some Halloween jokes,
As the beans tie themselves into knots - just some hoax.
The green brigade chuckles, they know they've got flair,
In this emerald lining, there's laughter to spare.

So let's celebrate greens, both leafy and sweet,
In the chaos of nature, there's joy with each treat.
From the sprouts to the vines, in their merry ballet,
Life's just a garden, come join the fray!

Imprints of Time in Green

In that corner of old, where the sun meets the shade,
A testament flourishes, a leafy brigade.
With stories embedded in every green crest,
The plants all conspire, and humor's the jest.

The lilacs whisper secrets to daisies so bold,
As they poke fun at the marigolds' gold.
The past laughs in petals, the deeds of the day,
While snails write their memoirs, in their own slimy way.

Old logs serve as benches for thorns and for thistles,
Where the ferns throw a party, complete with some whistles.
Time trickles like water, with nature so keen,
And the laughter runs deep in this vibrant scene.

So let us join hands with the trees and the breeze,
In the echoes of vines, we find laughter with ease.
The imprints we leave are a tale yet untold,
In the tapestry green, where humor unfolds.

Beneath the Sunlit Arch

Beneath the sunlit arch they play,
A friend with leaves on a sunny day.
One leaf on his head, quite a hat!
He twirls and stumbles, and that's that!

Through giggles and grins, he leaps around,
A dance with shadows, oh what a sound!
The bees join in, with wings like flares,
Declaring their buzz, they're the real players!

But wait! What's that? A butterfly flops,
Diving for nectar, while the laughter pops!
"Hey, keep it steady!" our friend yells with glee,
As he trips on a root, now he's stuck like a bee!

In costumes of green, the plants stand tall,
Making wisecracks, serving jokes for all.
The sun starts to set, it's time to retreat,
With leaves on their heads, they shuffle their feet!

Nature's Unveiled Palette

In a canvas where colors dance with cheer,
The flowers whisper jokes for all to hear.
A red poppy dares a bluebell to rhyme,
With petals in ruffles, they revel in time!

A squirrel flips once and lands by the rose,
"Can I borrow your shade?" in a voice that knows.
"I'll trade you some nuts for a sip of your dew!"
She giggles and blushes, a sight all too new!

The daisies debate, who's the best at pranks,
While tall grasses giggle, filled with leafy flanks.
A joke here and there, nature's comic show,
As the sun dips low, putting on quite a glow.

But hush now, dear friends, let the twilight sing,
For twilight holds secrets that laughter can bring.
In a world of colors, bright and absurd,
Nature's palette whispers, and giggles are heard!

Through the Lush Labyrinth

Through the lush labyrinth, a gnome appears,
With a high-pitched laugh, he banishes fears.
He trips on his shoe, then trips on his feet,
"Is this a maze or just my last meet?"

A rabbit darts past, with a wink and a hop,
"Keep up, little buddy, I don't wanna stop!"
Through bushes and blooms, they chase all around,
Finding the laughter in the soft, leafy ground.

But what do they see? A hedgehog in socks!
Rolling through daisies, collecting some rocks.
"With outfits like that, you belong on a stage!
Come join our parade, let's act like a page!"

With mishaps and chuckles, they dance in a line,
Each turn a new riddle, each bend a new sign.
So if you get lost in this vibrant terrain,
Just laugh with the greens, and you'll find your way again!

Quietude of the Grove

In the quietude of a grove so serene,
A squirrel holds court, he's the jester unseen.
With mischief and hops, he charms all around,
While chirps from the crickets compose joyful sound.

A fox with a scarf strolls in full style,
"Have you heard the latest? It's been a while!"
With tails that flick, they swap tales of glee,
As laughter erupts, from the grandest tree.

The wise old owl, perched high, gives a hoot,
"Let's play hide-and-seek; I'll count, you all scoot!"
As fawns bolt away, giggling full flush,
The dance of soft leaves adds to the hush.

And when dusk rolls in, painting night's hue,
The grove fills with whispers, a shared point of view.
In this silly retreat, where secrets hold sway,
Life's quirks offer joy, in the light of the day!

www.ingramcontent.com/pod-product-compliance
Lightning Source LLC
Chambersburg PA
CBHW070748220426
43209CB00083B/188